ROBOTS EXPLORING SPACE

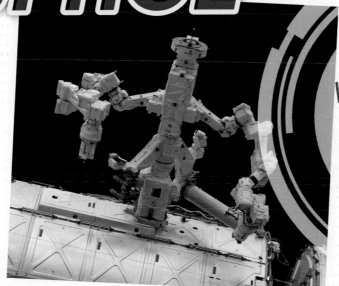

WILL ROBOTS TAKE OVER THE WORLD?

Louise Spilsbury

CHERITON
CHILDREN'S BOOKS

Published in 2024 by **Cheriton Children's Books**
1 Bank Drive West, Shrewsbury, Shropshire, SY3 9DJ, UK

© 2024 Cheriton Children's Books

First Edition

Author: Louise Spilsbury
Designer: Paul Myerscough
Editor: Jennifer Sanderson
Proofreader: Katie Dicker

Picture credits: Cover: NASA/JPL-Caltech (top), Shutterstock/Dima Zel/NASA (bottom).
Inside: p1: NASA, p4: Shutterstock/Sdecoret, p5: Shutterstock/KDdesignphoto, p6:
Shutterstock/Evgeniyqw, p7b: Shutterstock/Frame Stock Footage, p7t: Wikimedia
Commons/NASA, p8: NASA, p9: NASA, p10b: NASA, p10t: Shutterstock/M Aurelius, p11: NASA, p12:
Shutterstock/Aappp, p13: Shutterstock/Frame Stock Footage, p14: Shutterstock/Paopano/
Vadim Sadovski, p15: NASA/JPL-Caltech, p16: Shutterstock/Gorodenkoff, p17l: NASA/JPL-
Caltech, p17r: Shutterstock/OceanicWanderer, p18: NASA, p19: Wikimedia Commons/NASA,
pp20-21: NASA/JPL-Caltech, p20: NASA, p22: NASA/JPL-Caltech, p23: NASA/JPL-Caltech, p24:
NASA Kennedy Space Center/NASA/Glenn Benson, p25: JAXA, p26: NASA/JPL-Caltech/MSSS,
p27: NASA/JPL-Caltech, p28: Shutterstock/Supamotionstock, p29: NASA, pp30-31: NASA/JPL-
Caltech, p31: NASA/JPL-Caltech, p32: : Wikimedia Commons/DLR German Aerospace Center,
p33: NASA/Johns Hopkins APL, p34: NASA/JPL-Caltech, p35: ESA, pp36-37: Shutterstock/
Morrowind, p36: NASA/GSFC, p37: NASA/Johns Hopkins APL/Steve Gribben, p38: NASA/Johns
Hopkins APL/Steve Gribben, p39: NASA, p40: Shutterstock/Sdecoret, p41: Shutterstock/
Cowardlion, p42: Shutterstock/Willyam Bradberry, p43: NASA, p44: Wikimedia Commons/
NASA/Regan Geeseman, p45: Wikimedia Commons/NASA/Robert Markowitz.

Printed in China

Please visit our website,
www.cheritonchildrensbooks.com
to see more of our high-quality books.

CONTENTS

Chapter 1

ROBOTS IN SPACE

People have been gazing up at the night sky since the dawn of civilization, wondering what is up there in the vast inky darkness. Some humans have traveled into space but robots have traveled even farther. Today, robots are boldly going where no human has gone before. Robotic spacecraft and astronauts don't need to eat, sleep, or train. They can keep working all day, every day, with no fear of the dangers of life in space. Every year, more robots venture farther and farther out into space, to places humans cannot and dare not go. Maybe robots will one day take over space!

WHY EXPLORE?

People explore space for many reasons. They want to know what is out there, including the possibility of alien life. In space, scientists can get a clearer view of the universe than from Earth. Another reason to explore space is to discover resources, or things that we need. These include **minerals** that might be useful on Earth, and other planets that people might be able to visit or even live on in the future.

DANGER, DANGER!

Going to space is very dangerous for humans. In space, it can get incredibly cold and treacherously hot. Away from the rays of the Sun, temperatures can drop to far below freezing but in the sunlight, temperatures can shoot beyond boiling point. People are unable to breathe the air in space because there is virtually no oxygen. By staying inside a spacecraft and by wearing space suits, astronauts are protected from the dangers of space, but space travel is still very risky for humans.

SEND IN THE BOTS

Thanks to incredible technology, people can experience space, the planets, and other objects that float around **galaxies** far away without actually going there themselves. We can send robots in their place because they are able to survive space. Low temperatures and low oxygen? No problem for a space bot!

Could robots help us explore strange new planets in space?

BIG BOT DEBATE

Is Replacing Humans with Robots in Space a Good or Bad Idea?

Some people say space robots are a great idea. They argue that if something goes wrong, damage to or loss of a robot is far, far better than the injury or death of a human. They also believe that because robots are machines, they are less likely to make mistakes. But, others say we need to hold tight! They argue that at the moment, people still program and control the robots that are used in space, but if something went wrong and the robots took over they could cause havoc in space. Do you think space robots are an asset or do you believe they are a danger?

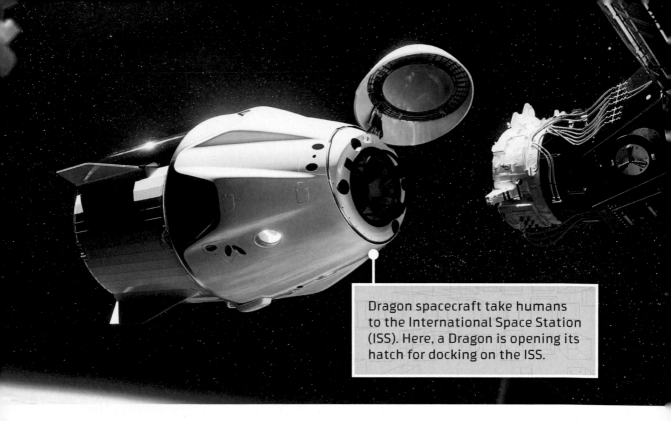

Dragon spacecraft take humans to the International Space Station (ISS). Here, a Dragon is opening its hatch for docking on the ISS.

ROBOTS ON SPACE STATIONS

The biggest human-made objects in space are space stations. These are giant **satellites** that move around Earth several hundreds of miles above the planet. Astronauts and scientists live and work alongside robotic helpers on space stations.

A STATION IN SPACE

The biggest space station is the ISS, which is about the size of a soccer pitch. The ISS was constructed in space from smaller parts, some for living in and others for carrying out experiments. The ISS has room inside for six sleeping quarters. It gets its power from massive **solar panels**. Scientists on the ground control the flight path of this huge station and the life support systems on board, which include the water and oxygen supply. They use **radio wave** signals to send instructions to the instruments on the ISS.

ROBOTIC CRAFT

Many visiting spacecraft have robotic controls that can guide themselves to the ISS and attach to the special docking ports on the side. They use **GPS navigation** to pinpoint their relative position. Computers compare the positions and instruct **thrusters** on the spacecraft to fire to gradually get it up close. Then, video-sensing devices take over to view the port and make sure the spacecraft is approaching correctly.

COME ON, CIMON!

The Crew Interactive Mobile Companion, or CIMON for short, is a roughly head-shaped, voice-controlled robot that can talk to astronauts on the ISS. It contains facial-recognition software so it knows who it's talking to. The robot can float around parts of the ISS independently and act as a hands-free **database**, computer, and camera to support astronauts.

A FLYING ASSISTANT

The ISS is large, and astronauts may sometimes have to work on a part of it alone. Imagine that you're an astronaut. Your hands are busy setting up an experiment but you suddenly have a question about the project you're working on. You don't want to have to stop what you're doing and move over to a laptop or call another astronaut to find the answer, before moving back to the experiment. This is where CIMON is useful. The astronaut can ask CIMON what to do next, without interrupting their work.

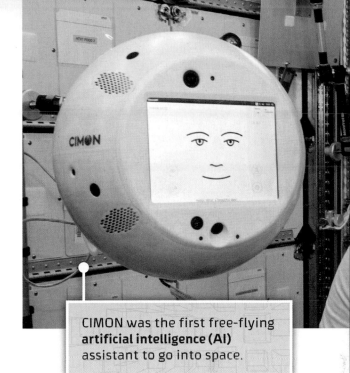

CIMON was the first free-flying **artificial intelligence (AI)** assistant to go into space.

ROBOTS RISING UP!

CIMON has a very simple design that allows the robot to show basic facial expressions on its screen. People view robots as less than human, so giving them a face makes it easier for people to communicate with them.

Imagine if, one day in the future, robotic assistants could help astronauts carry out their experiments in space.

7

Human work hours are precious and especially so in space. Astronauts have many tasks to complete and sometimes, they need help. Enter the Astrobees—three flying robots named Honey, Queen, and Bumble.

Taking Flight

Astrobees are cubes 12.5 inches (32 cm) wide. They fly and hover using electric fans. The fans point up, down, and to the sides, so the Astrobees can move in any direction. Astrobees navigate using cameras and sensors that detect, or sense, their surroundings. Computers control the fan operation, so an Astrobee can automatically avoid knocking into objects. Astronauts can program the robots to fly toward a particular location. When they're running out of power, the Astrobees seek and connect to a charging point to recharge their batteries.

Here to Help!

Astrobees are eager helpers. They may take photos of an experiment being carried out or go into a storeroom to find something. These robots can work alone but also in teams. They can fly in **formation**, for example, to support a large object. Their sensors make sure they don't knock into each other.

An Astrobee is a cube that is just a little bit wider than a ruler or vinyl record. This blue one is called Bumble.

Busy Bees

Astrobees can take care of maintenance on a space station when there are no astronauts on board. They are autonomous, which means they can operate and choose what to do on their own. Bumble uses its sensors and onboard computer to explore and create three-dimensional (3D) maps of a space station's interior. It can then patrol this area, on the lookout for tasks to do.

These Astrobees are flying in formation with an astronaut on the ISS.

BIG BOT DEBATE

On a Perch

An Astrobee has a fold-out arm, which it uses to grab one of the many handrails inside a space station, as if it's perching. Staying on a perch allows the Astrobee to save power it would otherwise use hovering, or remaining in one place in the air. The Astrobee can also assist an astronaut at that location.

Are Space Station Robots Helpers or Hindrances?

Some people think that having robots on a space station is very helpful. For example, they can carry out some routine tasks automatically and they stop astronauts from becoming tired when doing more important things. Others think they could be a hindrance and create too many problems. For example, a **malfunctioning** robot left alone on a space station might damage vital equipment, such as tanks carrying oxygen for astronauts to breathe. Do you think space station robots are helpful or do you think that they could cause problems?

ROBOTS GO OUTSIDE!

Working outside a space station is one of the most dangerous environments for humans. If they make just one false move, they could float off into space. If they damage their spacesuits, the air they need to breathe could escape. The robotic helpers on the outside of a space station limit danger to humans—they are the space station's arms.

POWER AND PRECISION

Robotic arms are made up of several parts, like human arms. They act as heavy lifters and maintenance crews. Robotic arms are connected, and move by using powerful electric rotating joints.

Sensors in the arm monitor how much it moves and with what force. Astronauts operating the arm can then feel, for example, how tightly to turn a bolt or how powerfully to grab a delicate item.

Completing tasks outside a space station is especially dangerous for human astronauts. Dextre can carry out many of their tasks, making space work much safer.

ROBOTS RISING UP!

Dextre is a robotic multi-tool. It has two jointed arms, each much bigger than a person's. Dextre moves across a space station, gripping as it goes. Once in position, it plugs into a power socket and does its jobs, such as changing broken parts or connecting cables. A camera and light on board lets astronauts see Dextre's every move.

Dextre and Canadarm2 work together to guide an approaching spacecraft to dock with the ISS. This is known as a cosmic catch.

BIG AND STRONG

Canadarm2 is the king of robotic arms. It works on the ISS and is 56 feet (17 m) long and around 14 inches (35 cm) across. It is hollow and made of tough **carbon fiber**. In Earth's **gravity**, it would not be able to support its own weight but in space's **microgravity**, Canadarm2 can lift the equivalent of an incredible eight school buses.

GRABBING HANDS

Canadarm2 has a grabber at either end. Cables inside tighten to give it a strong grip. The arm moves over the ISS end to end, a little like a looping caterpillar. Astronauts operate Canadarm2 using a joystick controller. Like Dextre, the arm plugs into different sockets across the station's surface for power and to link to the joystick controller.

SHIFTING THINGS ALONG

Canadarm2 can be used to move cargo, or goods, from visiting spacecraft onto the ISS. It can also connect new parts onto the space station. Canadarm2 can even safely hold an astronaut if they need to work on a distant part of the ISS, such as on its solar panels.

Chapter 2

ROBOTS IN ORBIT

There is a vast army of thousands of robots in space right now, orbiting, or circling, Earth. These are satellites. We rely on this team of robotic satellites for many things, from learning where we are and communicating with others on Earth to knowing more about our planet.

A RANGE OF ROBOTS

The robots in orbit range from tiny CubeSats, which are around the size of a softball, to those that are the size of a house. Whatever the size, all satellites quietly get on with their tasks. Those working in communication bounce data, or information, such as smartphone messages, or they stream TV shows from one point on Earth to another. Other satellites keep an eye on Earth, forecasting weather and checking that resources, such as forests, are not illegally destroyed.

Weather satellites are used to gather data on the heat, wind, and water in Earth's **atmosphere**.

Debris circling Earth poses a great threat to spacecraft and robotic missions.

Even a small bit of debris in space can cause silent-but-deadly damage as it hurtles through the darkness at high speed. Keeping track of debris and satellites is vital to avoid such damage. Satellites track where debris is in space, and so keep humans and their spacecraft safe.

ROBOT SWARMS

A group or swarm of robots in orbit can sometimes do a job better than a single satellite. For example, the swarm might provide better mobile Internet coverage on Earth. These satellites have sensors that record images of the nearby satellite. An onboard computer compares these images to a database of satellite shapes. The computer then calculates the direction, speed, and angle the satellite needs to take to move close to another satellite that is part of the swarm.

UNDER ATTACK

Space stations, satellites, and other robots in orbit are under fire, but these missiles are not shot from a gun. They are pieces of human-made space debris that accidentally orbit our planet. Flakes of paint chipped off a spacecraft, pliers an astronaut dropped, and old, broken satellites are all types of space debris that orbit Earth.

DEBRIS DUMPSTER

Robots in orbit can remove any damaged satellites and other space debris on their own. For example, Otter Pup has a device that can attach itself to the target and then give the debris a shove to push it out of orbit. Once it's out of orbit, the debris drops quickly into Earth's atmosphere. The **friction** when hitting air in Earth's atmosphere makes the debris burn up.

If orbiters spy on other planets and their moons from orbit, could they one day spy on us too?

WATCH AND LEARN

Some robotic spacecraft, called orbiters, are built to orbit distant planets and moons to study and learn more about them. These orbiters travel through space for thousands or even millions of miles and then spend years circling their target many times. Orbiters can fly farther than it is possible for humans to go at present, and they do a job that most people would consider very boring.

Cassini was a school bus-length robot that took 7 years to get to Saturn, which it then orbited for another 13 years.

LONG-DISTANCE ROBOTS

To get to their targets, orbiters have to travel enormous distances. They do this by using an electric motor that has solar panels to recharge batteries, and they follow a course programmed on their onboard computer. They also have flight systems that operators on Earth control.

ON THE LOOKOUT

Orbiters have sensors to detect which way up they are and to check they are on the right course. But their main purpose in carrying sensors is to learn in detail about a planet's features, such as size, temperature, and wind speeds. They transmit, or send, this data back to Earth using radio waves.

STAYING IN ORBIT

Why don't orbiters crash into planets? The force of gravity would normally pull a spacecraft toward the planet when it traveled nearby but robotic spacecraft remain at a particular height above a planet. For example, this might be far enough away to escape strong winds in a planet's atmosphere but near enough for sensors to "see" the planet in detail. Orbiters stay in orbit because they are moving so fast—they travel at many thousands of miles per hour. The faster something travels, the greater horizontal distance it covers as it falls. So the curve of its fall is far less steep than the curve of a much slower object.

ROBOTS RISING UP!

One of the most famous orbiters is Cassini. Its sensors allowed scientists to make remarkable discoveries about its target planet: Saturn. For example, they now know that Saturn has wind speeds four times greater than the fastest winds on Earth. Enormous **geysers** on a moon of Saturn send boiling-hot water high into the planet's atmosphere to create one of its ice rings. The geysers suggest that this moon has an underground ocean.

ROBOT TAKEOVER:
MOON LIGHTER

We can see Earth's moon at night, astronauts have visited the Moon, and many orbiter missions to the Moon have taken place. However, there is still a lot scientists don't know about Earth's moon. One of the latest missions for a robot in the Moon's orbit is simple: to look for ice on its surface.

Importance of Ice

Why do scientists need to know how much ice exists on the Moon? The answer is that there are plans to build a space station near the Moon and possibly **colonies** on its surface, where astronauts can live and work. In the far future, the Moon might even be a departure point for human missions to planets.

People cannot survive without water and oxygen to breathe. Rather than transport this to the Moon from Earth, it is better to make it from ice. Fuels for spacecraft for long-distance journeys through space can be made from ice, too.

Permanently Dark

On the dark side of the Moon there has been no sunlight for billions of years. At the colder south pole of the Moon there are deep **craters**, which are permanently in shadow and covered with water ice. To study the dark side of the Moon, scientists have developed the Lunar Flashlight. The Lunar Flashlight is a satellite the size of a briefcase or six CubeSats put together. Once orbiting, it will direct its sensors at the Moon's permanently dark regions.

Could robots help us one day live on the Moon?

BIG BOT DEBATE

Laser Power

The main tools on Lunar Flashlight are four **lasers**. These lasers emit, or give off, near-infrared light, not the visible light we see. The lasers shine on the dark parts of the Moon. A device called a reflectometer records how much light is reflected. More light is absorbed by ice, so less is reflected in these regions. Parts covered with rock or with dust will reflect more light. Using this data and data from other studies of the Moon, scientists will be able to map the parts that might be best to visit to collect water.

Are Orbiting Robots Safe or Dangerous?

Some people say that robots in orbit are very safe. They argue that robots can study a planet or moon from a safe distance rather than face a possibly tricky trip to land on its surface. It is much safer for a robot to do the orbiting rather than astronauts. Other people say that any orbiter could break and possibly become a dangerous piece of space debris. This would put manned missions at risk. Do you think orbiting robots are useful or do you believe they are a danger instead?

Chapter 3

ROBOT EXPLORERS

People have walked on Earth's moon but no humans have ever touched down on the surface of another planet. Instead, a group of robotic explorers is carrying out remarkable missions to distant moons and planets. These explorers have the technology to get close to unknown places and they are built to survive some of the most **inhospitable** worlds.

SURVIVING SPACE EXTREMES

Planets are not calm and peaceful places! Instead, they have storms, swirling winds, and ultra-extreme temperatures. The gravity of other planets also differs from Earth's—so hurtling through space and landing on a planet is not straightforward.

Landers are the robotic spacecraft designed to touch down on the surface of a moon, planet, or other space body. They must be tough enough to withstand the trip. They must also be able to protect the sensors and other exploration kit they carry from the damage of impact, or hitting the surface.

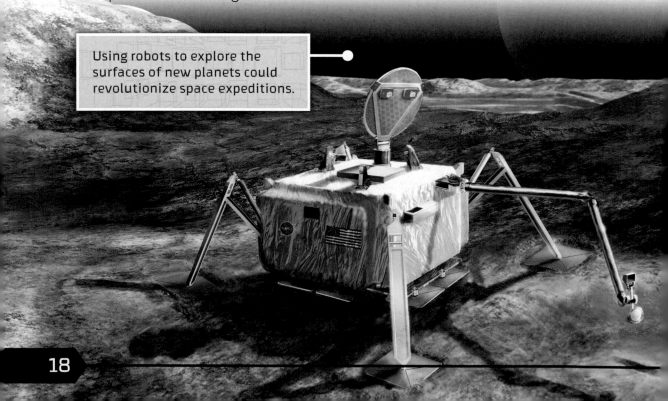

Using robots to explore the surfaces of new planets could revolutionize space expeditions.

When fully inflated, the 24 air bags that softened Pathfinder's landing looked like a huge bunch of white grapes.

A DANGEROUS DROP

When humans skydive, they use parachutes to slow their fall. Robots can do the same. Many landers slow their descent, or drop, through a planet's atmosphere by using tough parachutes. Some have jetpack platforms that gradually slow them, and they have shock-absorbing legs to help soften their landing on a planet's surface.

TOUCH DOWN

The Pathfinder lander was built to land on Mars. Pathfinder is fitted with airbags, which are similar to those found hidden in automobiles: They inflate, or fill with air, if the vehicle hits something. The round bags on Pathfinder are made from the same tough material as space suits and are designed to absorb the shock of impact on landing.

A few seconds before Pathfinder touched down on Mars, the airbags inflated all around the lander. After bouncing a few times and coming to a standstill, the bags deflated, or lost air, and the undamaged Pathfinder could start its mission.

ROBOTS RISING UP!

NOVA-C is a lander designed to land on Earth's moon. It has six sprung legs to land softly. Among its many onboard sensors is a two-lens camera. This will be able to take amazingly clear photos of things in space around the Moon, including the Milky Way galaxy. It has a drone camera that can fly past it and take videos of NOVA-C as it descends to the Moon. NOVA-C carries a drill to take **samples** of the ice beneath the Moon's surface.

THE ROBOTS ARE LANDING!

Landers are becoming more and more intelligent. They are being designed to work independently of humans by using powerful onboard computers. One day soon, they may be able to make decisions on their own.

LANDERS ON THE LOOKOUT

Eagles are birds that fly high and scan the ground below for food. Using this concept, scientists have developed a small robot designed to land on moons and **asteroids**. Known as Mighty Eagle, the lander can navigate autonomously, and fly on a preprogrammed flight path. If the Mighty Eagle spots a large target on the ground, it takes pictures, processes the images, and safely lands.

WHAT LIES BENEATH?

InSight is a circular lander with a mission to get below the Martian surface. It has a robotic arm to lift instruments off its back and onto the surface. Each instrument is attached by a special cord, a cable that supplies power and receives data from the instruments.

Mighty Eagle will make all the decisions about where to land on the Moon, when, and what to do next on its own, more than 217,480 miles (350,000 km) from Earth.

SMART TOOLS

One of InSight's instruments is a heat flow **probe** that burrows into the Martian soil to measure the temperature. The other is a seismometer that studies the movement of the ground. The instrument was the first to detect a marsquake—a violent shaking of the planet's surface that is similar to an earthquake.

ROBOTS RISING UP!

Robots seem indestructible but maybe they are not. At the end of 2022, the InSight lander was fighting for survival. NASA had lost contact with its lander when it failed to respond to communications from its control team. InSight suffered from power issues because of a build-up of dust from the surface of Mars on its solar panels. The dust stopped the panels from producing power InSight needed to keep going.

InSight has two circular solar panels to top up its batteries. The seismometer is on the left of the picture on the Martian soil and the probe is on the right.

ONE-WAY MISSION

There is no turning back for most space robots. They are on a one-way mission. The EDL lander gets its name from its mission: Entry, Descent, and Landing. Its job is to enter the atmosphere above a planet, move down through it, and land on the planet's surface.

Fast and Furious

Moving fast through space and then entering the atmosphere of gases around a planet is incredibly dangerous, even for robotic spacecraft. The reason is that the gases slow the movement, and the force of friction between gases and spacecraft produces heat. EDL deals with these issues by acting as a platform with its **rovers** held safely inside a heat shield.

Facing the Heat

EDL was released from a spacecraft above Mars. It then slowed down from 13,000 miles per hour (21,000 kph) to 1,000 miles per hour (1,609 kph) as it entered Mars' atmosphere. Although the temperature shot up to 3,800 degrees Fahrenheit (2,093 °C), EDL's heat shield carried out its job of stopping the intense heat from damaging the lander.

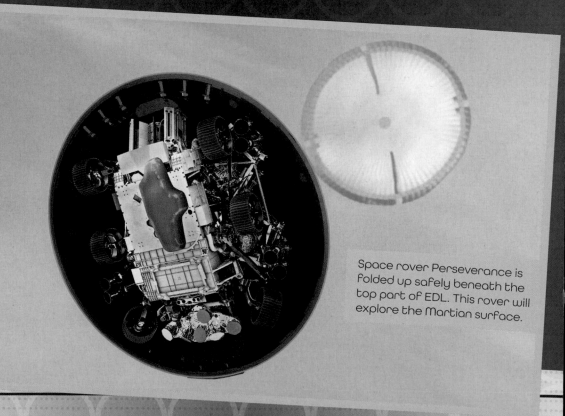

Space rover Perseverance is folded up safely beneath the top part of EDL. This rover will explore the Martian surface.

Held by powerful, strong cables, Perseverance was safely lowered onto the surface of Mars.

Dropping to Its Doom

EDL released a giant parachute to help slow its fall. Soon, its descent was down to a few hundred miles per hour. Then EDL detached its parachute in case winds on the planet blew it off course, away from its landing site.

The Point of No Return

At about 60 feet (18 m) above the planet's surface, EDL fired its eight downward-pointing thrusters. The downward blasts slowed EDL to a standstill and the rover was lowered on cables to solid ground. Then EDL flew off and crash-landed. Its mission was completed, and EDL no longer had a purpose.

BIG BOT DEBATE

Are Landers a Necessity or a Luxury That's Not Needed?

Some people argue that landers are the best way to get exploration robots onto planets. These robots can then do their valuable exploration and scientific research. Others say it is expensive and wasteful to build throwaway landers. They say that it is better to do more scientific research from spacecraft orbiting planets. Do you think landers are a necessity or do you believe they are simply an expensive luxury?

ROVERS IN ACTION

Most landers have simple missions: reach one spot on a planet and then stop. It is then time for other onboard robots, known as rovers, to take over and get to work.

MACHINES ON WHEELS

Many rovers are wheeled carts that move off their landers via folding ramps. The wheels have thick treads to provide grip when they roll over rocks and slopes, and to prevent spinning on dust. Rovers often have solar panels to power their instruments. Some rovers are driven remotely, or from a distance, by pilots on Earth. Others are autonomous.

USING SENSORS

Rovers are fitted with many sensors. Some onboard sensors can detect obstructions or obstacles the rover may have to steer around. Other sensors are all about studying the types of gases, rocks, and other features of the planet they are on. An **antenna** receives instructions and transmits data to Earth.

CubeRover has rugged, tall wheels, a power pack on its back, and sensors to find its way across planetary surfaces.

ROLLING ROVER

SORA-Q is a round rover that can drop from a lander and roll along a space surface, such as Earth's moon. It gathers data and images, and transmits these back to Earth. SORA-Q looks like the rolling bots in the Star Wars movies! The tennis-ball-sized rover splits open into two connected halves on landing. Each half is a wheel that can revolve in different directions to go forward, reverse, or turn. A tail drags in the dust behind to act like a **rudder** and makes sure SORA-Q does not topple over. The bar that connects the two halves when SORA-Q opens up, contains a flip-up camera so SORA-Q can see where it is going.

SORA-Q is a tiny, round rover that navigates the Moon. When a main lander reaches the Moon's surface, it will throw out rovers like SORA-Q, to begin their missions.

ROBOTS RISING UP!

After exploring many options, the SORA-Q designers realized that a ball represented the smallest possible shape. It's small and light but very tough for its size. It can even travel over sand without getting caught up, and moves and functions autonomously. Just imagine how far a swarm of these pocket-sized rovers could spread around the Moon!

Chapter 4

ROBOTS ON MARS

Mars is covered in poisonous dust and has an atmosphere of carbon dioxide, which is poisonous in large amounts. It is also bombarded with rays from the Sun and other stars. It's impossible for humans to explore this extreme and dangerous environment, but robots can. They are tough enough to survive and work on Mars.

SIGNS OF LIFE

At one time, people thought that aliens lived on Mars. Although today we know that isn't true, one of the main tasks of a Mars rover is to look for signs of life. For example, most living things on Earth are made partly from a substance called carbon. If a soil or water sample from Mars contains carbon, it could indicate that living things were once there. That is because carbon is often found in other substances such as methane, a gas that is produced as waste by living things on Earth.

Curiosity is a Martian rover that has been exploring the planet for more than 10 years.

TOOLS, TOOLS, AND MORE TOOLS

Martian rovers are bristling with all the tools they might need to study the planet. Many are held at the tip of a rover's robotic arm. The arm can lift this tool kit toward a rock or section of soil and put the equipment to use. The tools include:

- Spectrometer: to test the types and quantities of chemicals in Martian soil or rock

- Drill: to make holes in rock and produce dust samples to analyze

- Imager: the robot's version of a hand lens to give a detailed view of samples up close

- Sample analyzer: an instrument specializing in detecting carbon and other signs of life.

In movies, Martians often blast laser guns but robots can actually do that. Mars rovers have a special instrument that can fire powerful laser bursts at rocks up to 23 feet (7 m) away. The power of the narrow beam turns the rock into particles. These tiny pieces emit special light, and a telescope in the instrument then analyzes the light patterns to identify the chemical elements in the rock.

A rover's robotic arm is like a mobile laboratory that can operate many different specialist instruments.

LIFE ON MARS

One of the reasons humans are so eager to learn if the conditions on planet Mars once supported life is that they hope that we may live there, too. If this ever happens, scientists will be an important part of the new Martian working colony.

CONDITIONS FOR LIFE

The wish list for any robotic mission to Mars includes finding water, oxygen, metals, and other resources. On Earth, humans cannot survive without these, so it will be no different when they get to Mars. Rovers use their instruments to seek clues that these resources are there, even if they cannot spot them directly. For example, the shape of a crater might suggest an ancient lake, and grains of sand may be rounded if they were once worn down by running water. Special tools can analyze particles released from soil, which show that liquid or frozen water is underground.

LIVING CONDITIONS

The freezing Martian winters and violent dust storms are just some of the living conditions people would face. Robots are helping scientists learn what to expect when living there. Orbiters and rovers use spectrometers to examine the heat, gases, and dust in Mars' atmosphere. All of these things affect rainfall, winds, seasons, and other climate features. **Radiation** detectors can spot the type and amount of harmful radiation hitting Mars that could damage humans living there, too.

Imagine working alongside space robots to build colonies in space.

TOUGH ROBOTS

Robots can survive the extremes on Mars in ways humans cannot. For example, the Zhurong rover is like a **hibernating** animal—it can fold up its solar panels and go to sleep to save energy over the cold Martian winter. In spring, it can fold them out, power up, and go.

RASSOR is a robot with rotating, or turning, drums. It is used to excavate Martian soil.

ROBOTS RISING UP!

In the future, robotic miners could build places for humans to live and work on Mars. The red dust on the planet's surface contains many useful metals, such as iron and copper. It also contains silica, which can be made into glass-fiber, a useful building material. The RASSOR robot can be used to load, haul, and dump Martian soil.

ROBOT TAKEOVER:
DEVASTATING DUO

A devastating duo of new cutting-edge robots is moving around on Mars. One is a rover called Perseverance and the other is a drone known as Ingenuity. Their combined mission is to seek out signs of past or present life on the planet.

Mars Rover

Perseverance is around the size and weight of a small motor vehicle. It has six chunky wheels with very springy suspension. Perseverance has two identical computer units so it can always operate, even if one is not working. At the front of the rover there is a 7-feet- (2.1 m) long robotic arm with a tool kit at its tip for collecting and analyzing rock samples.

Non-Stop Explorer

A tall mast contains many separate cameras for spotting hazards, for driving, and for recording **high-definition** video as well as weather conditions. The rover and all of its instruments are powered using a **nuclear battery**. This also keeps the instruments warm so they do not stop working when it gets too cold.

Look and Find

Perseverance travels with its buddy: Ingenuity. This is a **rotorcraft** robot that flies like a helicopter but with two horizontal rotating blades and springy legs. Its mission is to scout for other locations so Perseverance can drive there and get to work with its scientific tool kit.

A Flying Scout

To achieve flight on Earth, wings or blades have to push against air but Ingenuity proves that controlled flight is possible on Mars where there is very little air. Ingenuity can fly there because it is very light, its helicopter-style blades spin very fast, and the blades spin in opposite directions. Robotic helicopters like Ingenuity could act as scouts for future planetary expeditions, too.

BIG BOT DEBATE

The Perseverance Mars rover is often known as "Percy."

Ingenuity has now made more than 50 flights over Mars' surface and proven that flight on a planet with little air is possible.

Are Rovers a Good or Bad Idea?

Some people say that robotic rovers are a great idea. They argue that these vehicles can explore inhospitable planets too difficult for astronauts to reach, operated by people many thousands of miles away, safe on Earth. However, other people think they are a bad idea. They say that as the robots drive over planets and grab samples, rovers could actually be destroying delicate signs of life. And what if they one day malfunction and do not share all the information they find with their human operators? Do you think rovers are a good idea or do you believe they are problematic?

Chapter 5

INTO DEEP SPACE

The toughest space robots can travel through deep space. The remarkable machines take on trips lasting many years, hunting down moving targets hundreds of millions of miles away. These targets often fly in big orbits around stars, so space robots need to organize their flight paths so they can meet up at the right time and place. Too early or too late, and the target they are chasing may have gone.

COMET CHASER

Rosetta took 10 years to reach **comet** 67P. It traveled nearly 4 billion miles (6.4 billion km), and looped around the Sun five times. It did this to gain speed by using the Sun's gravity and to put itself on an orbit similar to that of 67P. Rosetta finally caught up with 67P, which was traveling at 34,000 miles per hour (54,718 kph).

DELICATE OPERATION

Rosetta matched 67P's speed and path, then it released the Philae lander. Philae's harpoons failed to fire, so did not attach the lander to the icy surface of the comet. However, the lander still managed to take the first-ever photos of a comet's surface, and instruments were able to study the comet's ice. Mission partly accomplished!

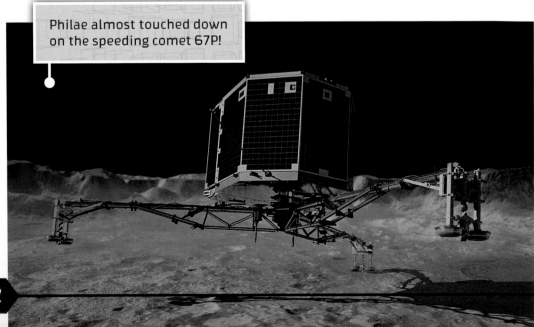

Philae almost touched down on the speeding comet 67P!

Dragonfly will fly from one place to another on Titan to get a complete picture of Saturn's moon.

TITAN-IC MISSION

A world mostly covered in water, with a nitrogen-rich atmosphere and many carbon-rich chemicals... This could be a description of Earth but it also applies to one of the moons in the rings around the distant planet Saturn. Robots will soon be exploring Titan's surface, searching for similarities to Earth. That will include water and possibly an ocean that is beneath the moon's surface.

DRAGONFLY ON DUTY

Dragonfly is a new rotorcraft robot that should arrive on Titan in 2034. This beast is huge and dwarfs Ingenuity! It will spend around three years on the moon. Once there, it will fly across the surface at about 20 miles per hour (32 kph) and reach altitudes of 2 miles (3 km). From up there, its cameras will help create an accurate 3D map of Titan's surface. Its sensors will analyze Titan's soil and underground rocks and water.

ROBOTS RISING UP!

The low winds and low gravity on Titan should make flight a breeze for Dragonfly. It uses eight spinning blades in four groups of two. Dragonfly can rise vertically from a standing start, fly, hover, and land.

BIGGEST OF ALL

Robots are targeting our solar system's biggest planet: Jupiter. This planet weighs far more than all the other planets combined, yet it is mostly made from swirling gases and liquids, rather than rock like Earth. The extreme temperature, pressure, and poisonous materials at and near its surface make life on Jupiter very unlikely. But this might be different on some of the 80 moons that orbit the planet.

UNDER ICE EXPLORER

Think of the incredible range of life in our planet's oceans. Three of Jupiter's moons are known to have underground oceans, like the one on Titan. It takes a special kind of robot explorer to visit underground oceans, especially those under frozen ground on distant moons.

SEEING IN THE DARK

BRUIE is the Buoyant Rover for Under-Ice Exploration. BRUIE has two large wheels with metal spikes along their edge. It will use these to grip and drive upside down underneath the slippery ice layer. This technology was proven on test trips to Antarctica. Just imagine the excitement on Earth when BRUIE powers up its cameras and lights so that scientists can see into the unexplored darkness of a moon!

BRUIE is a floating robot designed to explore oceans in deep space.

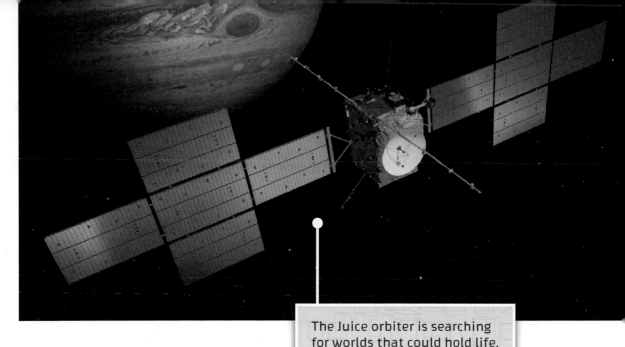

The Juice orbiter is searching for worlds that could hold life.

EXPLORING GAS PLANETS

Juice is a robot orbiter that was launched in 2023. Its mission is to get up close to Jupiter by 2031. Juice will carry more than its 2.6-ton (1.8 mt) weight in fuel to help reach its destination. Scientists working with Juice hope to understand giant gas planets better and to compare and contrast the three oceanic moons in greater detail than ever before.

DIVING INTO A SPACE OCEAN

One of Jupiter's moons, called Ganymede, may have a salty ocean like Earth's beneath its icy shell. Juice will use instruments such as radar to confirm what this ocean is made of, how wide and how deep it is, and what the ocean floor is like.

ROBOTS RISING UP!

A few weeks after launch, the Juice mission hit a snag. A radar antenna designed to see through the ice layer around Jupiter, failed to unfold from where it was safely kept on the robot. A pin holding it in place became stuck, so two-thirds of it remained folded. Scientists came up with a plan: They instructed Juice to fire up its engines to shake the pin loose!

ASTEROID ANTICS

The planets in our Solar System formed 4.5 billion years ago from an enormous disk of dust and gas. The remains of the dust and gas formed asteroids, comets, and other small worlds. Scientists think impacts between these remains and early Earth brought water and carbon-rich chemicals to our planet. This produced life on Earth. The clues to this process have been altered by weather and rock changes on Earth, but they might be intact on asteroids. Robots are searching for these clues.

OSIRIS-REx collected a sample from an asteroid hurtling through deep space.

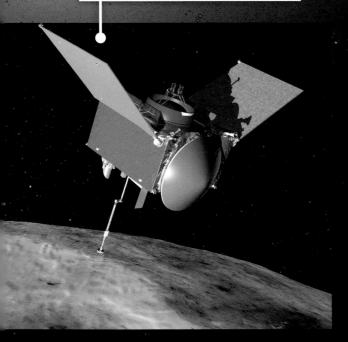

SPECIAL SAMPLES

The robot undertaking the first ever mission to collect a sample from an asteroid and return it to Earth was OSIRIS-REx. It launched in 2016, reaching the asteroid Bennu in 2018. It circled the asteroid while the mission team looked for a suitable sample collection site among the asteroid's boulders. In 2020, OSIRIS-REx flew down and unfolded its robotic arm to collect dust and pebbles from Bennu's surface. OSIRIS-REx packed the sample safely in a container and then started out for home. Scientists hope this sample will help them better understand how planets formed and how life began.

ASTEROID ALERT!

Asteroids can also be a threat to planetary survival. Millions of years ago, a collision of a 6-mile- (10 km) wide asteroid wiped out the dinosaurs. Scientists estimate there could be 25,000 asteroids big enough to cause major damage to our planet.

PLANETARY DEFENDERS

Don't panic! Robots in space will soon be on guard to help defend our planet from future asteroid strikes. One is a robot known as NEO Surveyor. NEO Surveyor has a telescope that specializes in spotting bright and dark asteroids, which many powerful telescopes on Earth struggle to find.

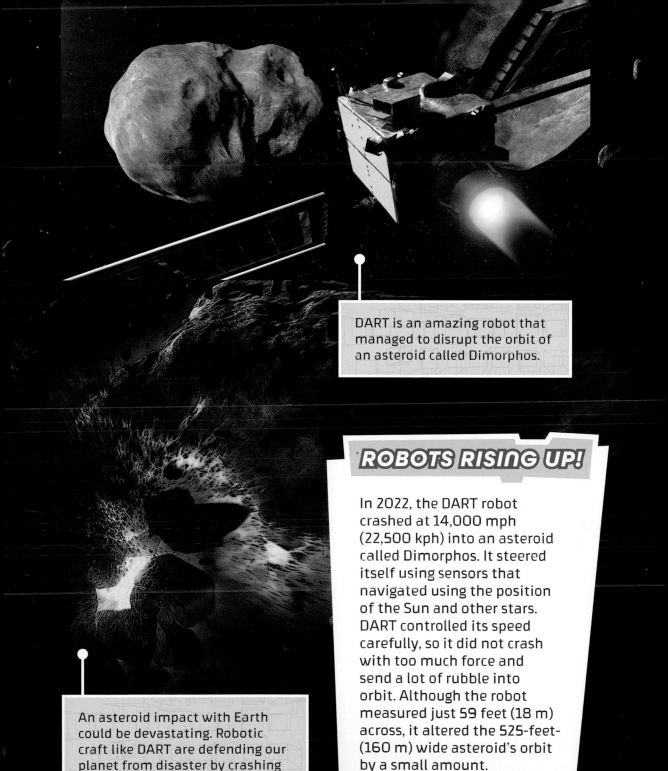

DART is an amazing robot that managed to disrupt the orbit of an asteroid called Dimorphos.

ROBOTS RISING UP!

In 2022, the DART robot crashed at 14,000 mph (22,500 kph) into an asteroid called Dimorphos. It steered itself using sensors that navigated using the position of the Sun and other stars. DART controlled its speed carefully, so it did not crash with too much force and send a lot of rubble into orbit. Although the robot measured just 59 feet (18 m) across, it altered the 525-feet- (160 m) wide asteroid's orbit by a small amount.

An asteroid impact with Earth could be devastating. Robotic craft like DART are defending our planet from disaster by crashing into asteroids and knocking them off their collision course.

If it's dangerous to look at the Sun directly from Earth, imagine how unsafe it would be to get up close to it. The dangerous radiation from this star could kill people any nearer than about 50 million miles (80 million km). But, robots can survive the Sun's intense conditions.

Built to Survive

The Parker Solar Probe goes closer to the Sun than anything ever before—close enough to touch the Sun's corona, which is the outermost part of its atmosphere. Parker operates in some of the most extreme conditions in deep space.

At 3.8 million miles (6.1 million km) away from the Sun's surface, temperatures reach nearly 2,500 degrees Fahrenheit (1,371 °C). The Parker Solar Probe is equipped with a 4.5-inch- (11 cm) thick shield to protect the probe's systems from the damaging heat. Underneath the shield, it remains at a more comfortable 85 degrees Fahrenheit (30 °C). The shield also blocks most light from hitting and destroying the delicate instruments.

The Parker Solar Probe touches the corona on the fly, orbiting at about 430,000 miles per hour (692,000 kph) around the Sun.

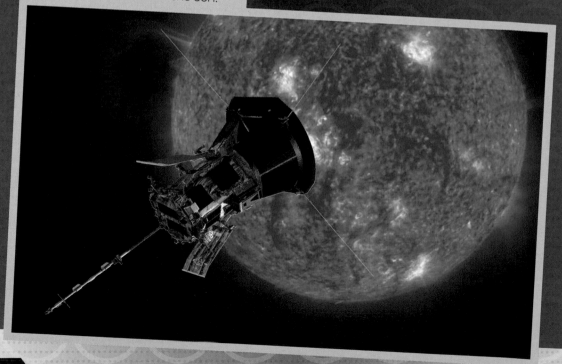

Mysteries of the solar wind are being unlocked by robots such as the Parker Solar Probe.

Secrets of the Corona

Humans cannot survive without the Sun's light and heat, so it is important that we understand what produces them. The main goal of the Parker mission is to unlock secrets of how Earth's closest star works. This robot's special camera is studying how energy and heat move through the solar corona.

Catching the Solar Wind

Parker also has a special electrical cup that catches, counts, and analyzes charged particles in the solar wind. Studying these particles has shown that the solar wind starts as jets from the base of the corona. Knowing about solar wind is important for humans because the wind affects Earth's climate. We also need to keep a careful eye on solar wind because it can interfere with the orbits and operation of space robots, which could affect future space exploration.

BIG BOT DEBATE

Are Star Probes Useful for Studying Earth's Climate?

Some people argue that solar probes are useful to climate study. For example, their instruments can unlock the secret of how the Sun makes light and influences our climate. Others say that they are a waste of money and the funds spent on these extreme expeditions should instead be used to deal with climate change. Do you think solar probes are useful or just a waste of money?

Chapter 6

ROBOTIC ASTRONAUTS

If you've ever dreamed of becoming an astronaut and going into space, you may face tough new competitors in the near future: strong, intelligent robotic astronauts that are always ready for action! Robots come in many shapes and sizes but future spacecrafts and space stations may be full of robotic astronauts that are humanoids. In other words, they look like human astronauts—with a head, eyes, arms, and legs.

ROBOTIC ASTRONAUTS HAVE THE EDGE

Humanoid astronauts have several advantages over their earthly competitors. Spacecraft and space stations are designed for human use. Robots shaped like humans can move around these spacecraft just as easily and use the same tools as human coworkers. Space is limited on all spacecraft and it is expensive to change or add features, so having humanoid robots that can function in existing spacecraft is a great advantage.

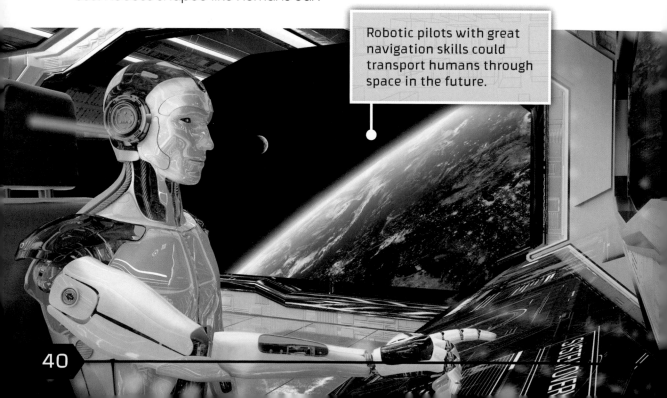

Robotic pilots with great navigation skills could transport humans through space in the future.

GETTING TO WORK

These tough, electric humanoid robots are capable of operating in some of the deadliest regions of space. Robots can help astronauts on long-range missions: They can communicate with humans, clean and repair craft, and they can act as caretakers of space stations when humans are not around.

ROBOTS RISING UP!

In 2013, a robotic astronaut named Kirobo became the first robot to speak in space. Kirobo's historic first words in space reflected the importance of this achievement: "On August 21, 2013, a robot took one small step toward a brighter future for all." Kirobo had a face and could talk but was much smaller than most humanoid robots.

TAKING OVER

Today, robotic astronauts use their skills to do dull, repetitive tasks. For example, working as a cleaner, wiping down surfaces and cleaning handrails, as well as doing other boring tasks such as checking air flow from vents. However, as humanoid robots develop, they will be able to do more complicated and important tasks in space.

A FRIENDLY FACE?

Humanoid astronauts are also designed to make human astronauts feel safer and more comfortable. Humans are more likely to think of humanoid robots as companions if those robots have faces. Some humanoid astronauts are even covered in a soft material so the robots feel less like a mass of metal and plastic. Many robotic astronauts can communicate with their human coworkers and are able to have a conversation with a human astronaut.

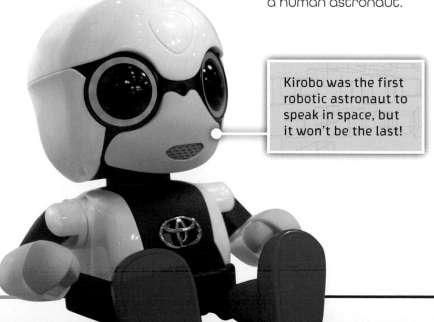

Kirobo was the first robotic astronaut to speak in space, but it won't be the last!

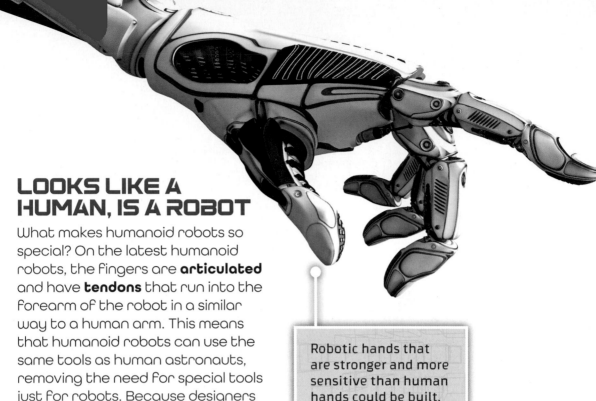

LOOKS LIKE A HUMAN, IS A ROBOT

What makes humanoid robots so special? On the latest humanoid robots, the fingers are **articulated** and have **tendons** that run into the forearm of the robot in a similar way to a human arm. This means that humanoid robots can use the same tools as human astronauts, removing the need for special tools just for robots. Because designers can decide how long and strong a robotic astronaut's limbs will be, they can choose to make its arms and legs longer and stronger. That means a robotic astronaut could reach farther and have a stronger grip than a human astronaut.

Robotic hands that are stronger and more sensitive than human hands could be built.

ASTRONAUTS IN ACTION

While the first robotic astronauts were given dull and boring jobs on spacecraft, this is set to change. Soon humanoid astronauts will be venturing outside a space station. Instead of feet, they can be fitted with clamping devices at the ends of their "legs." This means they will be able to grip tightly onto the handrails outside a space station to keep them from floating away into space. This also leaves their hands free to do important maintenance and repair jobs. They can be fitted with cameras in their feet, so they can see where they are going.

ONE OF THE TEAM?

Humanoid robots are getting better at communicating with people. They can be programmed to answer questions. The idea is for the humanoid robots to speak freely without input from humans. In the future, they may also be able to move their faces in a realistic way and can have an entire conversation with people.

INTO THE FUTURE...

As space travel becomes more difficult and dangerous for humans, it becomes more likely that space scientists will design robots capable of replacing human astronauts. If they do succeed in creating a humanoid robot with AI that can learn from and fully understand its surroundings, there would be no need for humans to travel on spacecraft to control or monitor such robotic astronauts.

ROBOTS RISING UP!

Perfect humanoid robots are difficult to make. Humans respond quickly to things going on around them, and make micro-adjustments to movements and activities. Programming a robot to do the same is a challenge. Despite that, space agencies worldwide are working hard to make more robotic astronauts.

Working outside a space station is incredibly dangerous. In the future, robots may carry out this work instead of humans.

Robonaut 2, or R2, is a humanoid robot. It's the size of an adult human in a space suit and it has a head, body, arms, and hands. R2 is designed to work alongside humans in space but one day, it may go farther into space and discover more than any human astronaut has learned to date.

Like a Human, but Better?

R2 has hands that move like human hands, so it is able to do tasks that could normally be done only by humans. When it first landed on the ISS, R2 simply took part in experiments to check its ability to push buttons, flip switches, and use tools that human astronauts normally operate. R2's arms are strong and its legs are about 9 feet (2.7 m) long.

Robot Senses

R2 has two cameras in its "eyes" that can see in 3D, just like human eyes. R2 also has an infrared camera in its "mouth," to sense how far away other objects are. It can move its head from side to side and up and down, so it can see all around. It is covered in force sensors that give it a sense of touch. If a human astronaut touches R2, it stops.

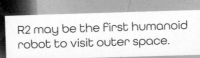

R2 may be the first humanoid robot to visit outer space.

Their Lives in Robot Hands

There are plans for R2 to act as a doctor to human astronauts. The idea would be that doctors on Earth could control R2 and instruct it on how to care for sick or injured astronauts on the ISS. Versions of R2 have already been trained to perform some simple medical tasks such as using a syringe to administer injections.

Robotic Astronauts Take Over

R2 is currently used only inside the ISS but there are plans to send it outside the station and even farther into space. If tests are successful, R2 and other robotic astronauts like it may even journey to planets far beyond our own Solar System in the future.

BIG BOT DEBATE

In the future, R2 might be able to ride on a wheeled rover and explore planetary surfaces.

Is Using Robonauts a Step Forward or Backward?

Some people say sending robonauts into space is a step forward. It saves putting human astronauts' lives at risk and robonauts are less likely to get tired or sick and make mistakes. Other people say it's too risky to let robonauts take over space. What if robonauts chose to take, rather than save, human lives or decide to take control of a space station altogether? Do you think using robonauts is the way forward or do you believe the risks are too great?

GLOSSARY

antenna a device that sends or receives radio wave signals

articulated describes something with several sections connected by flexible joints

artificial intelligence (AI) the power of a machine to copy intelligent human behavior

asteroids rocks that orbit the Sun

atmosphere the layer of gases around a planet

carbon fiber strong, light material made from strands of carbon

colonies places where settlers live

comet a ball of frozen dust, gases, and rock that orbits the Sun

craters hollows in the ground

database an organized collection of digital information, or data

debris pieces of garbage or remains

Formation an arrangement of things

Friction the force created between two materials when they move against each other

galaxies groups of stars and other objects bound together by gravity

geysers hot springs that erupt from under the ground

GPS an acronym for Global Positioning System, a system of satellites that work together to give exact locations on Earth

gravity an invisible force that pulls objects toward each other

hibernating sleeping or not moving over winter to save energy

high-definition very sharp and clear

inhospitable difficult to live in

lasers very narrow beams of highly concentrated light

malfunctioning not working properly

microgravity a very weak pull of gravity

minerals natural chemical substances that make up rocks

navigation finding and following a route

nuclear battery a device that makes electricity using heat made when atoms of special materials split

probe an instrument that collects scientific information

radiation energy given off in the form of waves or tiny particles

radio wave a form of radiation that can carry information

rotorcraft a machine that flies using one or several spinning blades

rovers spacecraft that can move across the surface of a planet or moon

rudder a flat device for steering a vehicle

samples small quantities of a material

satellites electronic devices placed in orbit around Earth to gather data

solar panels devices that absorb energy from sunlight and convert it into electricity

tendons flexible natural cables attaching muscles to bones

thrusters engines to push a vehicle or spacecraft in a particular direction

FIND OUT MORE

BOOKS

Owen, Ruth. *Space Robot Engineers* (Thrilling Science and Technology Jobs). Av2, 2020.

Sonneborn, Liz. *Space Robots* (Searchlight Books —Exploring Robotics). Lerner Publishing Group, 2023.

Thomas, Rachael L. *Revolutionary Robots in Space* (Cosmos Chronicles: Alternator Books). Lerner Publishing Group, 2019.

WEBSITES

Discover more about robots in space at:
https://spaceplace.nasa.gov/space-robots/en

Why should we send robots to space? Here are some answers:
https://science.howstuffworks.com/10-reasons-space-exploration-matters.htm

Watch a video about Curiosity's trip to Mars at:
www.youtube.com/watch?v=P4boyXQuUlw

Publisher's note to educators and parents:
All the websites featured above have been carefully reviewed to ensure that they are suitable for students. However, many websites change often, and we cannot guarantee that a site's future contents will continue to meet our high standards of educational value. Please be advised that students should be closely monitored whenever they access the Internet.

INDEX

ABOUT THE AUTHOR

Louise Spilsbury is an award-winning children's book author who has written hundreds of books about science and technology. In writing and researching this book, she has discovered that robots are rising, revolutionizing our world, and paving the way for an awesome high-tech future!